Celebrate James

participant guide

D1502726

wesleyan
publishing
house

Indianapolis, Indiana

Copyright © 2009 by Wesleyan Publishing House
Published by Wesleyan Publishing House
Indianapolis, Indiana 46250
Printed in the United States of America
ISBN: 978-0-89827-392-2

Contents

Celebrate Series Overview   4

Study Preview   5

Guidelines for Group Facilitators   7

1. A Believer's Unlikely Joy   9

2. Trusting through Trials   15

3. Wrestling with Temptation   21

4. God's Brand of Maturity   27

5. Fighting Favoritism   33

6. Why Faith Is Crucial   39

7. Becoming a Tongue Tamer   45

8. The Pursuit of Wisdom   51

9. Confronting Conflict   57

10. The Meaning of Life   63

11. Managing Money   69

12. Practicing Patience and Prayer   75

Celebrate Series Overview

The *Celebrate James* DVD and participant guide are part of a series of studies aimed to help people study and apply God's word and experience life transformation. Lessons are designed to be used in small groups but can easily be adapted for individual study.

The DVDs in this series feature the Bible teaching of Pastor Keith Loy. In each study, Pastor Loy will walk you through a book or books from the Bible, with a focus on helping you apply what you learn in a practical way.

Each participant guide contains study notes, as well as additional material to help you process and apply the teaching on the DVD. These include ideas for group sharing, connecting, and discussing, as well as action steps you can follow to implement your learning. You'll also find helpful instructions and guidelines for those who are facilitating small groups.

As you *Celebrate* and study the Word, whether as an individual or in a group, may God richly bless your life and help you grow in knowledge and obedience to our Lord Jesus Christ.

Study
Preview

If someone asked you to describe how trials and troubles result in joy, could you do it? It seems more reasonable that, if anything, trials snuff out joy. But in the upside-down kingdom of God, it's different. James puts it this way:

> Consider it pure joy, my brothers, whenever you face trials of many kinds, because you know that the testing of your faith develops perseverance. Perseverance must finish its work so that you may be mature and complete, not lacking anything (James 1:2–4).

This letter, written to believers scattered across the Roman Empire by James (probably the half-brother of Jesus), raises difficult questions about the external acts that mark those who serve the Lord. The connection between joy in trials and Christian maturity is but one case in point. Another is the control we have over one tiny part of our bodies: "If anyone considers himself religious and yet does not keep a tight rein on his tongue, he deceives himself and his religion is worthless" (1:26). Yet another is the relationship between what we say we believe and how we conduct ourselves in real time. James makes the bold challenge,

"Show me your faith without deeds, and I will show you my faith by what I do" (2:18).

Fasten your seatbelt. This won't be a study for wimps. It will challenge everything you thought you knew about living as a believer in Christ. But it'll be a healthy challenge that will leave you stronger in thought, word, action, and hope. And, of course joy.

In this DVD study of James, you will

- gain a broader perspective on how to approach setbacks and trials;

- come to understand how God is at work to grow you up into a mature believer who reflects his image to the world;

- become a more joyful Christian no matter what circumstances enter your life.

As you work your way through these twelve lessons, individually or as a group, may you be among those who, after having withstood the tests of life "will receive the crown of life that God has promised to those who love him" (James 1:12). Amen.

Guidelines for Group Facilitators

This DVD Bible study is designed as a *plug-and-play* small group experience, with little or no preparation necessary prior to each session. However, you'll find it helpful for your group to have a facilitator, someone who will manage details and guide the group's experience. Here are some helpful tips for those who serve as group facilitators.

SET THE ATMOSPHERE

Small groups should be casual, welcoming, and inclusive. Arrange a meeting place where people will feel comfortable and relaxed. Most often, this will be a group member's home, but it could also be a room in your church building that is specially equipped for this kind of meeting. Providing coffee, other beverages, and snacks can also contribute to a relaxed atmosphere.

ENCOURAGE PARTICIPATION

Make sure everyone has the opportunity to participate fully in your group. Invite different people to pray or read or provide refreshments. Also, be ready to give instructions like "This time let's hear from someone who hasn't spoken up yet" or "Jason, I'm wondering what you're thinking about this. Anything you'd like to share?"

KEEP ON SCHEDULE

This DVD Bible study is designed to take no more than ninety minutes for each session. Here is a typical schedule:

Welcome and Prayer	5 minutes
Share	10 minutes
Connect	15–20 minutes
Discover	10 minutes
Discuss	25–30 minutes
Implement	5–10 minutes
Wrap Up	5 minutes

As facilitator, guide your group through each step of the process and make sure they stay on track and on schedule.

Try to keep your meetings as positive as possible. Establish ground rules early on so that each person in your group is treated with kindness and respect.

Being a group facilitator does require a bit of extra time, but your servant leadership can make a big difference in the overall experience of the group.

A Believer's Unlikely Joy

JAMES 1:1–4

WELCOME and PRAYER
(5 minutes)

SHARE
(10 minutes)

*Take turns sharing what you hope
to gain from this experience.*

CONNECT
(15–20 minutes)

Although it was a steamy Sunday in mid-July, the sweat drenching the preacher's brow had little to do with the heat. Through red-rimmed eyes he looked over the congregation. His throat couldn't make any sound at first, but he finally found the strength to speak: "A life lived for Christ is not in vain," he began. The congregation wept through the sermon that honored his mother who had died the previous evening. He challenged them to make the most of their time; then he found himself strangely energized and holding back a smile. And he remembered the Scripture his mother had quoted often, "Consider it pure joy, my brothers, whenever you face trials."

Facilitator: Invite group members to participate in the following discussion.

Discuss how someone can find strength to exude joyful hope in desperate circumstances. Then take turns answering the following:

1. What's the difference between happiness and joy? Where does happiness come from? Where does joy come from?

2. When have you experienced joy although your circumstances were sad or bleak?

DISCOVER
(10 minutes)

Complete the study notes as you watch the DVD together.

Most scholars think James was the _____ of _____.

James doesn't say "_____" but "_____" troubles come your way.

Problems are _____, not _____.

Harry Sinden said, "It's the _____ of the players, not their _____, that is the biggest factor in determining whether you _____ or _____."

We're to rejoice _____ problems, not _____ them.

We're not _____; we're _____.

Immature people get _____, but patience is a source of _____ in the face of _____.

We need to develop _____ power—spiritual _____.

As far back as Genesis, those who worshiped God wholeheartedly were identified as servants of God. Even Jesus was identified as a servant by the prophet Isaiah (Isa. 42:1, 4). In a postmodern world where servant-hood is distasteful remember that God's Son came to earth to serve us—and he called us to serve each other (Mark 9:35).

God uses _____, not only to _____ us, but also to _____ us.

God's ultimate desire is that we become _____.

Christlikeness develops best in the _____ of _____.

If we value _____ more than _____, trials will _____ us. If we value the _____ more than the _____, we won't be able to "count

> *Joy is more than a momentary emotion tied to circumstances. It's a tenacious grasp on the truth that God is loving, gracious, and kind—and that he is at work in all circumstances to bring about our ultimate good and his ultimate glory.*

it a _____." If we live only for the _____, trials will make us _____ and not _____.

We must learn to evaluate every _____ in light of what God is _____, not what we're _____.

Your _____ will always determine the _____.

DISCUSS
(25–30 minutes)

1. James describes himself as "a slave of God and of the Lord Jesus Christ" (James 1:1). How do you think this self-understanding impacted his life? How does this help you make sense of his discussion about true joy?

2. Why do you think it's important for a follower of Jesus to face trouble with joy rather than complaint? What difference does your attitude make?

3. Do you think the troubles and trials James talks about are only to be understood as situations where Christians suffer specifically for the sake of God's kingdom? Or, does it apply to any kind of pain and suffering? Give reasons for your answer.

4. How do we reconcile James' instruction to face trials with joy to Paul's instruction to weep with those who weep (Rom. 12:15)?

5. Why is testing necessary to grow in endurance? What examples have you seen in your life or the lives of others?

> Bible commentator Matthew Henry said patience has its perfect work when "we bear all that God appoints, and as long as he appoints, and with a humble obedient eye to him."

6. How do people develop spiritual stamina? What are the benefits of developing spiritual stamina?

7. Pastor Loy says, "God uses trials not only to refine us, but to define us." How have you or others you know been defined by your trials?

8. James implies that endurance is part of having a strong character. Agree or disagree? Give reasons for your answer.

IMPLEMENT
(5–10 minutes)

Choose at least one activity to do before the next session. Tell one other person which item you chose.

1. Choose one or two verses from this week's session to memorize. Write them on a card and carry them with you to look at as you have time. Let the verses shape the way you think this week.

2. Take some time this week to think about the trials that you've experienced in your life. How have they helped you grow in endurance and character? Write about your experiences with trial in a journal or discuss them with a close friend.

3. Consider making it a habit to be joyful about the trials you experience. For the next twenty-one days, record every trial you face and thank God daily for each opportunity for growth.

WRAP UP
(5 minutes)

In the next session, Pastor Loy will show us how to apply what we've learned about the relationship between joy and trials to continue the process of becoming wise, mature believers. He'll encourage us to ask about each trial, *What is God trying to teach me?* To get a jumpstart, read James 1:5–12.

Trusting through Trials

JAMES 1:5–12

WELCOME and PRAYER
(5 minutes)

SHARE
(10 minutes)

*Take turns sharing what you learned
from applying the last session.*

CONNECT
(15–20 minutes)

When we think of suffering for Jesus, we often think of people who are beaten, tortured, and otherwise physically persecuted for their faith. It's true that many Christians in the world today who speak openly about their faith are in danger of real and violent persecution.

At the same time, we should not discount any of the troubles and trials we experience as a result of our faith, even though they may not rise to the extreme level of persecution. James indicates that everyone who follows Jesus can expect to experience testing. Rather than minimizing our own trials, we should approach them with hearts that are open to learn and grow in the ways that God intends for us.

Facilitator: Invite group members to answer the following questions.

What comes to your mind when you think of suffering for your faith? Why do you think that God allows people to suffer for their faith, instead of shielding them from it? Can you think of any ways in which you have experienced trouble because you have spoken to others about your faith? Tell the group what you have learned from such experiences.

DISCOVER
(10 minutes)

Complete the study notes as you watch the DVD together.

There is an island of _____ in the middle of every _____.

Success is a _____, not a _____.

God will never waste an opportunity to _____.

The great enemy of _____ is _____.

Fear is a _____ that causes extreme

_____.

Doubt creates _____, and _____

and _____ go hand-in-hand.

God wants us to be _____.

Double-minded means to be _____.

"He is the Rock, his works are perfect, and all his ways are just" (Deut. 32:4)

No matter what _____ we face, we must have _____ confidence that God knows _____.

One of the distractions to faith is _____.

> *In biblical terms, wisdom correlates with a clear understanding of God's big-picture work in the world. It calls on each individual to make a choice to live according to God's standards and in light of his purposes.*

Our _____ should never determine our

_____. Our _____ should never

determine our _____.

Social status will _____, financial wealth will

_____, and earthly fame will _____, but

a life that's _____ in Christ is _____.

First the _____, then the _____; first the _____, then the _____.

God doesn't _____ trials. He _____ us when we go through them.

> Sometimes we go about prayer all wrong. We ask to be delivered from a trial or test, rather than to be schooled by God's Spirit as we walk through the trial with him.

DISCUSS
(25–30 minutes)

1. Why is it so difficult to think about trials and challenges as opportunities or learning experiences?

2. James says that if you ask God for wisdom, he is eager to provide it. Do you think that there are conditions, limitations, or restrictions placed on this promise? Explain your thoughts.

3. Why do you think more people don't ask God for wisdom?

4. What is the role of doubt in faith? Is doubt always a bad thing? When, if ever, is doubt appropriate and when is it inappropriate?

5. Do you agree that doubt makes you indecisive? What examples can you share?

6. What role do you think material wealth and social status should play in our faith?

7. James says that Christians who are poor should be glad in their poverty and Christians who are rich should be glad when theirs dries up. How can this be? What does this say to us about the dangers of material wealth?

8. Pastor Loy notes that James writes first about "the cross, then the crown; first the suffering, then the glory. God is not about removing trials, but rather maturing us when we go through them." Can you think of examples of where Christians have pursued the crown and the glory without the cross and suffering? What are the consequences?

> *What a difference it makes to be reminded that the God of the Bible delights in giving the really valuable gifts of his presence, wisdom, grace, and love liberally to those who place our small, frail fingers into his all-mighty hand.*

IMPLEMENT
(5–10 minutes)

Choose at least one activity to do before the next session. Tell one other person which item you chose.

1. What are some decisions or areas of your life for which you need God's wisdom right now? Make a list and commit to praying for God's wisdom in

these matters every day for a week. Then be alert for the ways God might be speaking to you.

2. Examine your attitudes toward wealth and material possessions. What attitudes need to change in order to bring them in line with God's values?

3. Identify the people in your life that inspire faith in you rather than doubt, hope rather than discouragement. Make plans to spend time with one or more of these people before the next session. Or, be that kind of person for a friend who is currently struggling with doubt.

WRAP UP
(5 minutes)

While people and circumstances can certainly make it difficult to pursue a life in Christ, the biggest challenges to our faith often come from within. In the next session, Pastor Loy teaches us three key truths about temptation and three steps for finding victory over it. Before next session, study James 1:13–18.

Wrestling with Temptation

JAMES 1:13–18

WELCOME and PRAYER
(5 minutes)

SHARE
(10 minutes)

*Take turns sharing what you learned
from applying the last session.*

CONNECT
(15–20 minutes)

Monday. Staff meeting. Last Monday she'd succumbed . . . to French pastry. Giving in to that single impulse derailed her best intentions for healthy eating the rest of the week. Today, she renewed her resolve. She'd stick to her plan the entire week and be rewarded by feeling healthier and moving closer to her desired weight. But Monday loomed. As was his custom, her boss would stop at the bakery to bring in a chocolaty, buttery, gooey masterpiece of temptation that would sit in front of her the entire meeting. She looked at the tray on the passenger seat—a colorful array of fresh veggies. Could color and crunch outweigh chocolate goo through a morning of sales forecasts and reports?

Facilitator: Invite group members to participate in the following discussion.

Diet control is an obvious area of temptation for many people. That's why dozens of weight-loss gurus advertise day and night to attract devotees who are hopeful that this time they'll stick with plan X, Y, or Z. But what tempts you? Where are you most likely to give in to destructive thoughts and actions? Take turns talking about how you withstand temptation in big or small areas. Discuss what works and what doesn't work for you.

DISCOVER
(10 minutes)

Complete the study notes as you watch the DVD together.

Though God will at times _____ us, he never _____ us.

The source of our _____ comes from _____.

We're not _____ one minute and _____ the next.

Temptation begins in our _____. The birth-place of sin is in our _____.

What you think will eventually affect how you _____, and how you feel will eventually affect what you _____.

Fantasized _____ become factual _____.

We shouldn't give ourselves permission to _____ and _____.

> Bible scholar Warren Wiersbe says, "When you realize how good God is to you, you will have no interest in the temptations the enemy puts before you."

Unchecked _____ yields sin. Unconfessed _____ brings forth death.

The first step in dealing with temptation is to find _____.

The second step is to _____ our minds.

People have a choice about where they allow their _____ to _____ and _____ they play there.

The difference between testing and temptation is vast. Testing of faith may come from God through the difficult circumstances of life. This leads to being purified and shining brighter for God. But temptation to commit evil does not have its source in God—because he has no communication with evil.

Fenelon said, "We are not masters of our own _____, but we are, by God's grace, masters of our _____.

The mind is a powerful _____, and it must be _____ and _____ wisely.

You will _____ like you _____.

The third step in dealing with temptation is to fix our _____.

DISCUSS
(25–30 minutes)

1. Jesus taught his followers to pray, "Lead us not into temptation, but deliver us from evil" (Matt. 6:13 KJV). How does that prayer connect with James' teaching about temptation in verses 13–14?

2. In a culture that claims man is basically good on the inside, what does it mean to believe and apply James' teaching that temptation comes from evil desires within us?

3. Why does James make such a big deal about the human tendency to blame God for the evil in our world—and in our lives? What difference does it make who is to blame?

4. James teaches that evil desires come from our sin nature, but good gifts come from the heavenly Father. How can we consistently reject the evil desires and embrace the good gifts?

5. What comfort do you find in the unchangeableness of God—especially in light of your old sinful nature?

6. The new birth James talks about in verse 18 sounds a lot like the new birth Jesus offered in John 3. Why do we need new birth? How does it equip us to fight temptation?

The firstfruits of each harvest were offered to God as a thanksgiving for the bounty he provided. They were an acknowledgement that these good gifts come from his hand. When we're called "firstfruits" as believers in Christ, it reminds us that the good gift of salvation from his hand ought to elicit our gratefulness.

IMPLEMENT
(5–10 minutes)

Choose at least one activity to do before the next session. Tell one other person which item you chose.

1. Write an action plan to deal with the temptation that besets you most often. Decide how you will stand against it. Make it a matter of daily prayer that God will equip you with his power to turn away from temptation and choose his better plan for you.

2. Meditate each day on the fact that God, the creator of everything and the lover of your soul, never changes. Express your thankfulness to him for deciding to give you life through his word of truth.

3. Make a list of every gift you've ever received from God. Post this list on your desk or mirror or dashboard—someplace where you'll see it many times a day. Add to it as you receive new gifts from his hand.

WRAP UP
(5 minutes)

Next session we'll wrap up this first chapter of James with a discussion of three principles of Christian maturity. As you prepare to open your ears to what God will say to you on this topic, read James 1:19–27. Look especially for the key principle of *listening*, which recurs throughout the passage.

God's Brand of Maturity

JAMES 1:19–27

WELCOME and PRAYER
(5 minutes)

SHARE
(10 minutes)

*Take turns sharing what you learned
from applying the last session.*

CONNECT
(15–20 minutes)

The professor sat down for an informal chat with his student's mother. Her son, just out of high school, had good intentions, the professor said, but didn't grasp the opportunity before him. The freshman had a vague sense that he was enrolled in classes to be educated— when it was convenient and didn't interrupt his social plans—but his intensity was lacking. The mother acknowledged that her son was much like she had been at that age. Yet, she now wished for another opportunity to pursue a degree. The professor excitedly

> The apostle Peter provides a wonderful reminder that immaturity early in a person's journey with Christ doesn't preclude our future usefulness. Peter was impulsively immature many times as he walked with Jesus, yet eventually Jesus honored this loyal follower with the responsible, mature call to "feed my lambs" (John 21:15).

told the mother that if she should ever want to put feet to that wish, he'd sponsor her for admission into an adult diploma program.

Facilitator: Invite group members to participate in the following discussion.

Looking back at your younger days, take turns describing opportunities you took lightly then that you now wish you'd taken more seriously. How has maturity changed you?

How deep are your roots in Christ today? How well could your Christian life sustain the harsh environment of a desert period?

DISCOVER
(10 minutes)

Complete the study notes as you watch the DVD together.

James gives us three principles for Christian maturity—be quick to _____, slow to _____, and be _____ to God's Word.

When our mouth is _____, our ears are _____.

Since God gave us two _____ and one
_____, we should _____ twice
as much as we _____.

Steven Covey says that one of the
habits of success is "seeking to
_____ before seeking to
be _____."

> According to Easton's
> Bible Dictionary, "It is a
> great paradox in Christianity
> that it makes humility the
> avenue to glory."

Slow down. _____ is an enemy to listening.

Looking a person in the eye says, "_____."

Listen for that which is not being said. Approximately
_____ percent of conversation is _____.

Will Rogers said, "People who fly into a rage seldom make
a good _____."

Alexander the Great said, "I've conquered the _____,
but cannot conquer my own _____."

Anger is a _____. No one can force you to
_____.

Thomas Jefferson said, "If you're angry, count to
_____. If you're really angry, count to
_____."

Anger is a _____ of something deeper.

God wants to move us from being _____ of the
Word to _____ to the Word.

_____ makes one godly.

DISCUSS
(25–30 minutes)

1. What elements of active listening challenge you
   the most? Why is listening often called "the lost
   art"? How do you feel when someone really listens
   to you?

2. How can truly listening to one another help us
   work through conflict and dissension at home, at
   work, or at church? Why do you suppose James
   equates being a good listener with Christian
   maturity?

3. How or why do you think unbridled anger demon-
   strates personal immaturity?

4. Pastor Loy reminds us that anger is a choice.
   How is this true? Why are we tempted to place
   the blame on others when we fly into a rage?

5. What is the connection between expressing anger
   inappropriately and the presence of sin within us
   (v. 21)?

6. In the Bible, humility is often tied directly to a person's depth of relationship with God. Discuss why this is true. Explain why humility is necessary if a person is to choose to obey God.

It was the expression of unbridled anger that caused the world's first heinous act of murder: Cain's killing of his brother Abel back in Genesis 4. Cain wasn't just angry with Abel, he was angry with God because of his standard of perfection.

7. Why is knowing the right thing to do in any given situation insufficient in itself? What else is necessary for the mature believer in Jesus Christ?

IMPLEMENT
(5–10 minutes)

Choose at least one activity to do before the next session. Tell one other person which item you chose.

1. Read the book of James in one sitting. List all the actions James says true believers will take. Choose three of those concrete actions to work on this week. Note what you learn about being a *doer* of the word.

2. Choose an elder family member or friend. Make an appointment to sit with him for an hour. Prepare questions about family history, faith, or something else that's important to him.

Begin by asking one of those questions—then use your best active listening skills.

3. Journal about the difference between the sufficiency of faith in Christ to save us and the evidence of true faith, which James says is found in the works that mark a believer's life.

WRAP UP
(5 minutes)

Not only does Christian maturity show itself in a proper view of ourselves before God, but it also shows in a proper view of our relationship with others. We'll look at the sin of favoritism next session, from James 2:1–13. You can prepare you heart for the next session by studying those verses prayerfully.

Fighting Favoritism

WELCOME and PRAYER
(5 minutes)

SHARE
(10 minutes)

Take turns sharing what you learned from applying the last session.

CONNECT
(15–20 minutes)

The pivotal character in George Bernard Shaw's *Pygmalion* is the Cockney flower girl, Eliza Doolittle. When the story opens, Eliza is a comfortable-with-herself working girl who fits well in the street society she was born into. But phonetics professor Henry Higgins, who sees her as a means to his own ends, changes all that by dressing her in pretty clothes, working her to the point of exhaustion on phonetics, and making a proper British lady out of her. The problem is that once he's finished with his noble experiment, Eliza neither fits into high society nor her previous community. Her old friends don't even recognize her. The same girl is at once neither flower-seller nor lady of leisure—yet she's treated differently by all.

Facilitator: Invite group members to participate in the following discussion.

Take turns answering the following questions:

- If you've ever seen *Pygmalion* or the adaptation *My Fair Lady*, describe how you felt as Higgins treated the lower-class Eliza like a laboratory experiment rather than an equally valuable human being.

- If Higgins, the old Eliza, and the new Eliza were to walk into the room, which would you feel most comfortable befriending? Why?

DISCOVER
(10 minutes)

Complete the study notes as you watch the DVD together.

Everybody _____ in the household of God.

What's the point of _____ church if we're not going to _____ the church?

"If you love only the people who _____ you, you will get no _____" (Matt 5:46 NCV).

We should make _____ according to God's standards.

"People look at the _____ of a person, but the LORD looks at the _____" (1 Sam. 16:7 NCV).

When we exploit the poor, we _____ God.

If we're serious about living like Christ, we must _____ people as he _____ and not as we _____.

A class church has no _____ at all.

When Jesus died, he broke down the walls between _____ and _____.

The royal law says to love our _____.

> Most people tend to associate with others of similar race, age, and financial state; those who speak the same language, those with whom they have the most in common. But God established his family out of every generation, every nation, every financial strata, and every level of political and social influence.

Neighbors are anyone in _____.

We only _____ as much of the Bible as we _____.

While the passage is addressing partiality in the church, it could as well apply to partiality in the home. One look at the damage caused in Jacob's household by his mother's favoritism of him and his father's favoritism of his brother Esau reminds us that equality in treatment is as needed among blood siblings as among siblings of faith.

D. L. Moody said, "Every Bible should be bound in _____.

We must be careful with our _____.

Just as important as words are our _____.

We don't earn _____ by showing it. We _____ mercy because that's what we're called to do.

DISCUSS
(25–30 minutes)

1. How is the demonstration of favoritism a transgression of the command: "Love your neighbor as yourself" (Matt. 22:39)?

2. Describe God's standards of judging as opposed to the standards used by the world. What is the danger of judging based on externals? What is the danger of assuming we know what's in another person's heart?

3. James suggests that it's a small step from favoritism to exploiting someone we consider lower in status. Why does God find this offensive?

4. Scripture says we were destitute spiritually or dead in sin without Christ. How ought God to have treated us? What did he do instead? How does this challenge you to change your view of others— such as the homeless, poor, infirm, or aged?

5. Assuming a Christian's words and deeds could be seen as reflections of the master, what would a watching world observe about God by watching how the church confronts favoritism? How accurate would their view of God be?

6. Good works—in this case mercy—are a common theme in James. Discuss the paradox that while works don't save us, good works like showing mercy are required of us. What's the role of good works in the believer's life?

> *In Colossians 3:12–13, Paul equates mercy with kindness, humility, gentleness, and patience—with how well we get along with each other and whether we forgive each other.*

IMPLEMENT
(5–10 minutes)

Choose at least one activity to do before the next session. Tell one other person which item you chose.

1. Go to a local nursing home. Ask the staff which residents seldom have visitors. Then spend an hour with at least one person the staff names.

Listen to his stories. Comb her hair. Wheel him to the social room. Read to her. Find some appropriate way to serve the person.

2. Volunteer to serve in a soup kitchen or homeless shelter. Be careful of your attitude—that you don't think of yourself as better than those you're serving. Rather, look for the face of Christ in each person you serve.

3. Find out about your community's after-school programs. Ask what you can do to help the organizers. Perhaps you could tutor or bring snacks or tell stories to entertain the kids.

WRAP UP
(5 minutes)

This week we've focused on the outward expressions of service for Christ through joy, good works, and lack of favoritism. We'll turn our attention next session toward an internal subject: faith. We'll discover the balance between what we say we believe and how we live out that faith in everyday life. In preparation, read James 2:14–26.

Why Faith Is Crucial

JAMES 2:14–26

WELCOME and PRAYER
(5 minutes)

SHARE
(10 minutes)

*Take turns sharing what you learned
from applying the last session.*

CONNECT
(15–20 minutes)

Walk through the parking lot toward the door of any grocery store or shopping mall between Thanksgiving and Christmas, and you'll hear them. Well, you'll hear them if you listen. They're such a staple that it's more common to tune them out than to listen. But they're there . . . tinkling bells that announce Salvation Army ringers collecting money from in-the-season revelers to fund charitable endeavors in needy communities around the globe. A few nickels here. A few dollars there. It adds up. When Christmas is over, most of us forget about the Silver Bells. But not the Salvationers. One Salvation Army worship center posted this invitation on its marquee in January: "You know what we do . . . Come inside to find out why."

Facilitator: Invite group members to participate in the following discussion.

The connection between good works and faith has sparked many debates and great division among those who claim Christ—including the Reformation. But it's more than theory—it's practice. Take turns discussing how an unbeliever might interpret the deeds you (individually) and your church (corporately) do week in and week out.

DISCOVER
(10 minutes)

Complete the study notes as you watch the DVD together.

Faith is not believing in spite of _____, but obeying in spite of _____.

The first key to distinguishing between real and counterfeit faith is _____ versus _____. It's the difference of one letter—_____ and _____.

People need to _____ what we _____.

James gives us a second key identifier: If you
_____, you will _____.

Real faith is more than just
_____; it's _____.

> Faith carries with it the connotations of loyalty and allegiance, in addition to a confident belief in something that may not be provable empirically.

The third identifier is: _____
versus _____.

Faith is more than _____ knowledge. Real faith
is _____.

The final identifier is: The proof is in the _____.

Both Abraham and Rahab exercised a _____
faith.

There is a perfect relationship between _____
and _____.

Dynamic faith _____ God and _____
itself in daily living.

Abraham and Rahab did not see faith as something to
_____, but as something to _____
in response to God.

Since you gave your heart to Jesus, what _____
can you point to in your _____?

Is your _____ any different than before?

What would others say is most _____ in your life?

DISCUSS
(25–30 minutes)

1. Talk about specific actions that Christians can take every day or every week that will prove to someone watching that we believe in Christ. What does real faith look like?

> Bible commentator David P. Nystrom says the connection between faith and works that James describes has to do with "fidelity to the call of Jesus" and integrity, which he defines as, "becoming an integrated person, one in whom beliefs and actions are linked."

2. Explain the difference between a religion made up of a list of *dos* and *don'ts* and a faith that is evidenced by actions.

3. What is the danger in judging others (or ourselves) by our actions? What is the danger in divorcing faith itself from the visible evidence of faith (good works)?

4. Why isn't it enough to just say you believe in God and his Son Jesus? What more is necessary?

5. How does sharing—both among fellow believers and with a needy world—give evidence of faith?

Conversely, how does hoarding reflect negatively on the God we serve?

6. What was it about Abraham's life that caused him to be described as "God's friend"? How might a modern-day friend of God behave?

> Claiming a secure faith, grounded in the living God who made our salvation possible by his gift of grace, places each of us in the position of becoming willing to act as his ambassadors. This role requires that we work in his name as his representatives to a world that doesn't know him.

7. Grapple with verse 24. Do you believe James is saying that we can buy salvation with our works? Or do you believe he is saying something else? If so, what? Support your position with your knowledge of other passages in the New Testament.

IMPLEMENT
(5–10 minutes)

Choose at least one activity to do before the next session. Tell one other person which item you chose.

1. Which area of connecting faith and good deeds do you struggle with the most? Journal your thoughts and commit your struggle to God in prayer.

2. What is one tangible deed you can do that would represent Christ well? Do that deed—not looking for personal gain, but to give Christ glory.

3. Since sharing has to do with both sharing earthly goods and sharing your faith, look for ways to do both at least once this week. First, locate a reputable charity or family that can benefit from something you have to give. Separately, share your salvation story with someone who doesn't know Christ and offer him the opportunity to accept the gift of salvation.

WRAP UP
(5 minutes)

Actions are only part of the bigger picture of how we represent Christ. The words that come out of our mouths play a major role in how the world views the veracity of our professed faith. That's the subject we'll tackle next session, when we look at James 3:1–12. Read that passage in preparation for the session, and pray about what you discover.

Becoming a Tongue Tamer

JAMES 3:1–12

WELCOME and PRAYER
(5 minutes)

SHARE
(10 minutes)

Take turns sharing what you learned from applying the last session.

CONNECT
(15–20 minutes)

Her blood shot to the boiling point as the five-year-old sassed her. Seeing the little figure before her with her arms on hips and her face set defiantly, the mom let loose with a vocal assault: "Don't you dare defy me, young lady. This is not a democracy—and it's not a debate. Now you'll do as I say or you'll be sorry!"

She was mid-holler when the cell phone rang. She moved her own hands off her hips, grabbed the phone, and checked the number. The pastor. Wouldn't you know it? Her withering look held the little girl suspended in time as she flipped open the phone. "Well hello, Pastor. How nice to hear from you. I was just praying for you . . ."

Facilitator: Invite group members to participate in the following discussion.

Think about the mother-daughter scene we've just read, then take turns filling in the blanks below:

- Someone made my day when he or she said _____ to me.

- Someone hurt my feelings when he or she said _____ to me.

- As soon as I'd said _____, I wished I could take it back.

DISCOVER
(10 minutes)

Complete the study notes as you watch the DVD together.

Our tongues may be _____, but they can get us in all kinds of _____.

"What you say can _____ life or _____ it" (Prov. 18:21 GNT).

We've got to learn to _____ our tongues.

Our _____ is vital to our Christian _____.

"Those who _____ their tongue will have a long life" (Prov. 13:3 NLT).

Commentator David Nystrom writes, "When the tongue is influenced by the forces of hell, the result is severe double-mindedness. This irrationality is seen in that the same tongue may praise God but curse people, who have been made in God's likeness"

_____ does not equate with _____.

We may think our words are insignificant, but one _____ can change a life _____.

Intelligent people understand the _____ of words.

_____ does not equal _____.

A tongue may be _____, but it packs an enormous _____.

"A quarrelsome person starts _____ as easily as hot _____ light charcoal or _____ lights wood" (Prov. 26:21 NLT).

_____ should not contradict _____.

Whatever is on the _____ will eventually come to the _____.

If our talk is going to match our _____, then we have to get our _____ right before God.

The tongue may be _____, but it has great _____.

DISCUSS
(25–30 minutes)

1. Why are teachers held to a higher standard? How do James' statements about the tongue relate to the statement about teachers in verse one?

In the Middle East during New Testament times, salty sea water was easier to find than drinkable water. So, natural springs that burst from deep within the earth were not only refreshing, but life-giving. Equating these springs with the patterns of speech befitting Christ followers created a vivid picture for the original readers.

2. In Matthew 12:36 Jesus said, "Men will have to give account on the day of judgment for every careless word they have spoken." How do you think Jesus defines "careless words"? Why did he make a big deal about speaking rightly?

3. Grapple with what does and does not constitute proper speech for a Christian. For example, does it include swearing? Staying away from certain topics? Restraining angry outbursts? What else?

4. Why should we find it troubling when we notice bitter and pure speech coming from the same mouth? Why ought we to be suspect of sweet words from a salty mouth?

5. James makes a bleak statement in verse 8: "No man can tame the tongue." Do you believe this? Why or why not?

> The Bible mentions the tongue in several contexts, often in reference to its sharpness, its poisoned words, its deceit, and its use in backbiting, cursing, and creating destruction. But in Luke 6:45, Jesus reminded his listeners that the mouth speaks what comes from the heart—either evil or good.

6. Keeping with the theme of fresh water springing from somewhere down deep, what is the source of proper speech for a Christian? Consider Jesus' promise in John 4:14.

IMPLEMENT
(5–10 minutes)

Choose at least one activity to do before the next session. Tell one other person which item you chose.

1. In your journal, list the times you use your tongue to tear someone down or speak careless words. Also list the times you use it to build someone up. Examine your list, confess before God the times you've sinned with your tongue, and praise him for the times you used your tongue wisely.

2. Go to someone you've offended through rash use of your tongue, and apologize genuinely. If you have trouble finding the words to do this, read Psalm 51 and make it your spoken prayer before God.

3. Consider how your words and actions have an impact on the words and actions of others. Ask God for grace to cover times when you falter and for his fountain of life-giving water to bubble out from you.

WRAP UP
(5 minutes)

Next time we'll return to a subject we touched on briefly earlier, God's brand of wisdom. We'll see how it differs from common sense and even from the pursuit of knowledge. We'll also discover its one and only source. To prepare yourself for this session, read James 3:13–18.

The Pursuit of Wisdom

JAMES 3:13–18

WELCOME and PRAYER
(5 minutes)

SHARE
(10 minutes)

Take turns sharing what you learned from applying the last session.

CONNECT
(15–20 minutes)

He told them to rest the land every seven years. But it seemed to them a waste to let good land sit idle. Now we know that crops draw nutrients out of soil and eventually deplete it. Resting the land yields a greater volume in the end. Likewise, God told them to take a day off once a week. But it seemed to them a waste to let a good work day go idle. Turns out workers who rest are more productive in working hours. From this vantage point, many seemingly pointless directives God set for his people turned out to be wise counsel from the creator who knew them, their bodies, and their world inside out.

Facilitator: Invite group members to participate in the following activity.

Take turns listing as many items as you can that God would consider signs of wisdom but that the world would call ill-advised. Then, using that list, discuss how God's value system differs from the world's and why his system ultimately yields immeasurably greater rewards.

DISCOVER
(10 minutes)

Complete the study notes as you watch the DVD together.

"Teach us to _____ the most of our _____, so that we may _____ in _____" (Ps. 90:12 NLT).

Trivia is not God's _____. God wants us to gain _____.

Wisdom enables us to use _____ rightly.

According to James a *walking* Christian is characterized by a _____ life.

A *talking* Christian is one who _____ only of _____.

"But if you have _____ and _____ in your hearts" (James 3:14 ESV), there's something wrong.

Ever since the garden our _____ bent has been to trust in _____.

James gives us the complete _____ for wisdom.

James tells us wisdom is _____. The word *pure* means _____ and _____.

Wise people seek _____.

James tells us that wise people never _____ another's feelings.

> According to Nelson's Bible Commentary, "The Old Testament meaning of peace was completeness, soundness, and well-being of the total person. . . . In the New Testament, peace often refers to the inner tranquility and poise of the Christian whose trust is in God through Christ."

Wisdom is also open to _____.

If you're wise you don't rub things _____, you rub them _____.

These two words in Greek, *impartial* and *sincere*, mean "without _____."

Wisdom begins and ends with _____.

In answer to young Solomon's request for wisdom, God rewarded his search by gifting him with an immense supply of wisdom. We can tap into a little of that supply by regularly visiting the book of Proverbs.

"If you become _____, you will be the one to _____. If you scorn _____, you will be the one to _____" (Prov. 9:11–12 NLT).

DISCUSS
(25–30 minutes)

1. How does verse 13 relate to topics we've examined before, like faith and works? What does James' return to the theme of wisdom do to enhance your understanding of living a life of good deeds?

2. Compare and contrast the markers of "unspiritual" wisdom listed in verse 14 with the markers of godly wisdom listed in verse 17.

3. Turn to Galatians 5:22–26. How does Paul's list corroborate James' list? How do the two lists fit together to help you understand how to apply this abstract concept to real life?

4. How would you define wisdom in light of what you've read in this passage? What's the difference between earthly wisdom and "wisdom that comes from heaven" (v. 17)?

5. How can jealousy and selfish ambition become particularly damaging within the body of Christ? How can these traits undermine wisdom?

6. How do traits like "peace-loving" and "peace-makers" demonstrate godly wisdom? What is it about peace that leads to the kind of living James called us to?

> Peter ties the antidote to ills like envy and evil speaking to filling ourselves up on the "pure milk of the word" (1 Pet. 2:1–3). As God's Word is the ultimate source of wisdom for believers, Peter's reminder is worth heeding.

7. If someone asked you how to become *wise* and *understanding*, what action plan would you offer to help him or her reach that goal?

IMPLEMENT
(5–10 minutes)

Choose at least one activity to do before the next session. Tell one other person which item you chose.

1. Using the lists in verses 14 and 17, find at least one other Scripture passage that mentions each trait. Pay attention to what other Bible writers say about them. Then, draw conclusions on how you will live as a result.

2. Ask God to point out specific areas where you are deficient in his wisdom. Ask him to show you where you are harboring envy or selfish ambition or a lack of humility. If he points to an area, be quick to confess it to him and seek his wisdom in breaking free of it.

3. Equipped by God's Spirit and guidance, seek out a situation within your realm of influence where a peacemaker is needed. Approach the situation prayerfully, but confidently that God will honor your efforts with his wisdom.

WRAP UP
(5 minutes)

We'll follow up on the peacemaking aspect of James' challenge in our next session. We'll dig into the subject of harmony within the body of Christ. Read James 4:1–12 to prepare your heart, and look specifically for the antidote to disunity that James lays out for us.

Confronting
Conflict

JAMES 4:1–12

WELCOME and PRAYER
(5 minutes)

SHARE
(10 minutes)

*Take turns sharing what you learned
from applying the last session.*

CONNECT
(15–20 minutes)

It seemed such a small issue, offering loans to folks who wanted to own bigger and better homes. So what if the loans were larger than the folks could pay back comfortably? Incomes would rise. Property values would rise. They always had before. Except that they didn't this time. Property values fell. Homes were worth less than people owed on them. Homeowners defaulted. They also stopped buying cars and large appliances and taking extravagant vacations. Banks that made loans and kept other folks' savings failed. Employers initiated layoffs and companies filed for bankruptcy. It didn't take long for financial markets to tumble worldwide. Such is the interconnectedness of twenty-first-century economy—when one small element is unhealthy, it affects the health of all.

Facilitator: Invite group members to participate in the following discussion.

The same kind of interconnectedness that can cause global financial crisis can wreak havoc on relationships—especially relationships within God's family. Take turns discussing how you have seen quarrels within and among churches affect the health of the whole body. How do internal conflicts affect new believers? Seekers? Children?

DISCOVER
(10 minutes)

Complete the study notes as you watch the DVD together.

"It is good and _____ when God's people live together in _____" (Ps. 133:1 NCV).

James gives us both the _____ and the _____ to every _____.

The war of the _____ is the greatest war of all.

"If any of you wants to be my _____, you must put aside your selfish _____" (Matt. 16:24 NLT).

_____ is Satan's great sin, and it's one of his chief _____.

If we're going to get along with others, we must first start with _____.

Submit means "to yield to the _____ or _____ of another."

We tend to _____ what we hang around.

> "God's people, wherever they live on earth, are linked into a grid of community interdependence from which they can never escape. Inextricably bound to one another as separate parts of the whole, what affects one becomes part of all."
>
> Speaker's Sourcebook
> of New Illustrations

"The sacrifice God wants is a _____ spirit. God, you will not reject a heart that is broken and _____ for sin" (Ps. 51:17 NCV).

Sin breaks our _____ with God and wreaks havoc on our _____.

Admission of sin is the mark of true _____. Far better that we _____ ourselves before God than we be concerned about the _____ of men.

DISCUSS
(25–30 minutes)

1. Explain how evil desires within individual believers can become the bane of the entire church. How can something so personal, so hidden, and so small take on public consequences?

> *Humility is a true view of ourselves in God's eyes—seeing ourselves as dependent on God, the provider of every good and perfect gift.*

2. How does acting on covetous thoughts lead to even more consequential sins? When we have a strong desire for something, what does James tell us we ought to do about it? Why?

3. How does the accusation in verse 3 lead you to think differently about prayer—and about your prayer life?

4. If someone is making the choice between friendship with the world and friendship with God, how would you suggest the person take the first step toward God? What does God want from his people?

5. Why does God require humility of those who would have him draw near to them? What do you suppose it means when he promises he will lift up his humble servants?

6. What particular damage does slandering a fellow believer do to the whole body? Why is it a big deal?

> Coveting is more than just wanting something someone else has. It's obsession, an ache or craving that becomes the center of all thought. Covet despises the one who has what it wants, and it schemes the other's destruction so it can possess for itself.

7. What happens to us when we judge someone? Read Romans 2:1–3 and 1 Corinthians 10:15. Discuss when it might be appropriate to judge and when it definitely isn't.

IMPLEMENT
(5–10 minutes)

Choose at least one activity to do before the next session. Tell one other person which item you chose.

1. With your Bible open to James 4, tell God you want to choose friendship with him over friendship with the world. Listen as he prompts you with sins that stand in the way of your relationship with him. Repent and seek his help in overcoming them.

2. Find every Scripture you can on humility and journal what each adds to your understanding of it. Then journal about the person you now realize you are before God.

3. Review your prayer list. Paying special attention to prayers that haven't yet been answered, put them to the measure of James 4:3. Ask: What are my motives? What do I plan to do if God answers affirmatively? Am I seeking my pleasure or God's glory?

WRAP UP
(5 minutes)

Next session we'll broach a huge topic that bridges philosophy, science, and theology: The meaning of life. James has something fresh to say to us as we consider why God has placed us here in time and space. Read James 4:13–17 to prepare for the discussion.

The Meaning of Life

JAMES 4:13–17

WELCOME and PRAYER
(5 minutes)

SHARE
(10 minutes)

*Take turns sharing what you learned
from applying the last session.*

CONNECT
(15–20 minutes)

The time slot between late night talk and early morning news is the realm of the infomercial. From clearer skin, to healthier bodies, to miracle kitchen toys, gurus hawk 'em all for just $19.95 plus shipping. Flip beyond these innocuous ads to find the get-rich-quick-and-I'll-tell-you-the-secret offers. Just invest a little money, and they'll give you the secret to making a six-figure income by only working ten hours a week. They trade on our greed. For the least possible expenditure, we want—no need—to collect and hoard as much stuff as we can. Preferably more than our neighbors, so they can be jealous of our financial acumen. But don't you wonder how futile this all looks from God's vantage point?

Facilitator: Invite group members to participate in the following discussion.

Since boasting about how much we have, what we'll do tomorrow, and how much we'll succeed is a human tendency, take turns discussing times when you have fallen prey to this. How did pride about your success take on greater proportions when you bragged to someone else? How and when did you cross the line into foolish boasting?

DISCOVER
(10 minutes)

Complete the study notes as you watch the DVD together.

Zig Ziglar asks, "Is our life a wandering _____ or a meaningful _____?"

"For I know the plans I have for you," says the LORD. "They are for _____ and not for disaster, to give you a _____ and a _____" (Jer. 29:11 NLT).

First, consult God on _____.

There's nothing wrong with making _____.
Solomon wrote, "Good planning and hard _____
lead to _____" (Prov. 21:5 NLT).

"We can make our _____, but the LORD
determines our steps" (Prov. 16:9 NLT).

The statement, "if it's the Lord's will," should be a constant
_____ of the heart.

The second thing James tells us is
never _____ tomorrow.

Every one of us is a _____
away from _____.

"LORD, remind me how _____
my time on earth will be. Remind me
that my days are _____
and that my life is _____
away" (Ps. 39:4 NLT).

> The picture of Jesus bowed and sweating drops of blood in Gethsemane provides us with the greatest encouragement to submit willingly to God's purposes, even when it is most painful. If our master subjugated his will to the Father's, how much more ought we acknowledge his right to select our paths?

Boasting is only a cover up for _____.

Finally, "Anyone, then, who knows the _____ he
ought to do and doesn't do it, _____" (James
4:17).

You can do three things with your life—_____ it,
_____ it, or _____ it.

> "Everything which to vain men seems to happen in nature by accident, occurs only by [God's] Word, because it happens only at His command."
>
> —Augustine

"He is no _____ who gives what he cannot _____ to gain that which he cannot _____" (Jim Elliott).

DISCUSS
(25–30 minutes)

1. How would you define the meaning or value of life? What measure do you use? What measure do you believe God uses?

2. How does the boast of the merchants in verse 13 relate to the earlier statement that God requires humility from those who seek him? In what ways does their pursuit demonstrate that they hold different values than God?

3. What do you do when an unforeseen tomorrow (with illness, a loved one's death, being disappointed by a close friend or family member) accosts you? Where do you turn? Why?

4. When life feels overwhelming, as if pressures will never let up, how can the reminder that "you are a mist" be a comfort? In what circumstances might that same statement become an indictment?

5. How do you seek the Lord's will? When you find it, what motivates you to submit to it? How often do you need to be reminded to do this?

6. What does Pastor Loy's statement that you can do one of three things with your life "spend it, waste it, or invest it" challenge you to do or to become? Consider this in light of verse 17.

IMPLEMENT
(5–10 minutes)

Choose at least one activity to do before the next session. Tell one other person which item you chose.

1. Whether or not you say it aloud, preface every decision and plan you make this week with the statement of the early Christians: *Deo valente,* "If God wills." Note what difference this reminder makes in your plans.

2. If you have long-range goals written down, get them out during a quiet moment with the Lord. Set them before him and invite him to change them to fit his priorities for you (rather than asking him to bless the plans you've made).

> "Happy is he who, once for all, has made the firm choice, and every morning renews the choice, not to seek or listen for feeling, but only to walk by faith, according to the will of God."
>
> —Andrew Murray

The Meaning of Life

3. Using James' reminder that "you are a mist that appears for a little while and then vanishes," do a thorough evaluation of how you're spending your life, your energies, and your resources. Consider the good you ought to do and then do it.

WRAP UP
(5 minutes)

Agreeing to submit our plans and dreams to God's will is only part of the prescription for becoming a joyful Christ follower. Next session we'll consider one of the most controversial and touchy elements of living as a believer: Our use of financial assets. Read James 5:1–6 prayerfully as you ready your heart for the discussion.

Managing Money

JAMES 5:1-6

WELCOME and PRAYER
(5 minutes)

SHARE
(10 minutes)

Take turns sharing what you learned from applying the last session.

CONNECT
(15–20 minutes)

Only rarely does a local story make national news, but this one did. For the first time in history, a sitting governor of the state of Illinois was impeached by the State House and removed from office by the State Senate. Local TV stations broadcasted gavel-to-gavel coverage. Weeks earlier the governor had been arrested in the early morning hours after a long investigation by the state prosecutor. The state prosecutor produced tapes on which the governor purportedly was heard attempting to sell to the highest bidder a vacant U.S.

Senate seat. While it could take years to prove or disprove charges, the indictment raised issues of wealth, how it was acquired, and how others were treated in its acquisition.

Facilitator: Invite group members to participate in the following discussion.

> The believer can take away from this passage a reminder that someone sees and will call us to account for our actions.

It's not only politicians who acquire and use wealth in questionable ways. Discuss how the temptation to gain wealth through dishonest or shady means can haunt the most upright people. Take turns listing public instances you recall when there were similar allegations to those against the Illinois governor. How did these stories color your impressions of the individuals involved and their professions?

DISCOVER
(10 minutes)

Complete the study notes as you watch the DVD together.

Money, in and of itself, is not _____. The problem begins when we _____ it more than God.

Whatever accumulates _____. There's only one _____ that lasts.

It's okay to hold wealth in your _____ as long as it is not permitted to get into your _____.

Just as dangerous as _____ on to wealth is, so too is how we choose to _____ it.

"Do not . . . take _____ of anyone. Do not hold back the wages of someone you have hired, not even for one night" (Lev. 19:13 GNT).

As Christians, we are called to deal _____ with one another.

"Those who love _____ will never have enough. How absurd to think that _____ brings true _____!" (Eccl. 5:10 NLT).

> Because Christ loves people, he is angered when those who claim his name misuse people in the pursuit of wealth. Think of his response to the money-changers in the Temple: "'My house will be called a house of prayer,' but you are making it a 'den of robbers'" (Matt. 21:13).

Unrighteous gain has a way of ruining good _____.

It doesn't take long for the _____ of money to replace our _____ for others.

Affluence is a _____ to invest, not a _____ to impose.

James didn't condemn _____ or the _____; he condemned the wrong _____ of it and the _____ in getting it.

DISCUSS
(25–30 minutes)

1. Why can the pursuit of money become so dangerous? What is it about money that tempts people to worship it—to put it ahead of everything and everyone else?

2. How do you define wealth? How did you come about that definition?

3. What is your gut response when James claims "Your wealth has rotted . . . Your gold and silver are corroded" (v. 2)? When the stock, bond, or real estate market turns downward, how does a person who trusts in wealth respond? How does a person whose treasure is in heaven respond?

4. The statement, "You have hoarded wealth in the last days" sounds like it's been drawn from any day's newspaper. How do you find comfort in the fact that God knew days like these would come? How does this challenge your behavior and thought patterns?

The tone in this section of James becomes accusatory and prophetically condemning. It's a frightening warning to those who want to please God in all their dealings.

5. Why does God consider it a breach of trust when a manager mistreats employees?

6. How will God ultimately judge those who use unethical methods to gain wealth at the expense of others?

> The word translated as "indulgence" and "luxury" carries with it the connotation of debauchery. This is not a little over the top. It's wanton maliciousness and unrestrained excess used for one's own selfish wants.

7. What does God require of the one entrusted with wealth? What directions can you glean from this passage and from Pastor Loy's comments that govern a good manager's use of wealth?

IMPLEMENT
(5–10 minutes)

Choose at least one activity to do before the next session. Tell one other person which item you chose.

1. Read the conversion of Zacchaeus (Luke 19:2–10). Consider how the former cheater responded to coming face-to-face with Jesus. Journal your observations and the conclusions you can draw for yourself.

2. Review your net worth in dollars and cents. Ask yourself, "How much is enough?" Open it all to God as you approach him in prayer. Invite God to reveal places you are honoring him with your finances and places where you may be dishonoring him. Act on what he shows you.

3. Consider the Proverb: "One man gives freely, yet gains even more" (Prov. 11:24). No matter how much or how little you own, look for ways you can give freely to those in need. Don't give expecting to get something in return. Give because it will bring honor to God.

WRAP UP
(5 minutes)

Many of us are uncomfortable facing the issue of patience in our own lives. We often give in to the dominant message of our culture that you can have whatever you want and have it now. James broaches the topic of patience in our next session. Read James 5:7–11 to see what he has to say on this touchy topic and to prepare for the next meeting.

Practicing Patience and Prayer

JAMES 5:7–20

WELCOME and PRAYER
(5 minutes)

SHARE
(10 minutes)

Take turns sharing what you learned from applying the last session.

CONNECT
(15–20 minutes)

Watch any Olympic sporting event where individuals compete to go farther, faster, longer, or higher, and you'll see people who have trained their bodies to do things only a comic book hero ought to be able to do. Jump off a mountain and fly two hundred feet. Or perform a flawless quadruple toe loop on an icy rink. Or use a pole to propel over a precarious bar. How do they get to the point where they're able to perform these feats? More than body type or a vague inclination of wanting to be an athlete, there is only one way world-class athletes get to this stage: patience. They practice, whether they feel like it or not, over and over. They fall. And they get up to try again.

Facilitator: Invite group members to participate in the following discussion.

If you've ever participated in athletics, discuss your experience of patience as you learned to compete in your sport. Since patience is just as necessary in every other discipline—including our personal maturity and faith development—each person take a turn telling how patience has been integral to at least one success in life.

DISCOVER
(10 minutes)

Complete the study notes as you watch Session Twelve Part One of the DVD together.

James teaches us about our need to be _____ in the face of _____.

We live in a _____, and it will never be _____ until the Lord returns.

Life is no _____ or _____ in the park.

We are going to face _____, but we are to patiently _____.

How many _____ have fallen short because someone failed to go one _____ further or hold on one _____ longer?

As we wait, we will _____.

Following Jesus doesn't mean a life of _____ and _____.

As we wait, we are never _____.

Patience precedes _____. Blessings will come but at the _____. If we want all the _____, then we must be prepared to carry the _____.

Job is the poster child of suffering. He lost his _____, his _____, and his _____. From the outside, he looked _____. But on the inside, he was growing _____. Job didn't understand his _____, but he completely understood his _____.

The passage speaks of both patience and perseverance. Where patience carries the idea of calmly waiting and expecting God to work, perseverance requires that we do something as we're waiting— that we push through the circumstances to continue accomplishing God's purposes despite difficulties, opposition, or delay.

The will of God will never _____ you where the grace of God cannot _____ you. We can hold _____ because he will always hold _____.

DISCUSS
(25–30 minutes)

1. When you hear the phrase, *Jesus is coming soon,* how do you respond? What significance does James' instruction to "be patient . . . until the Lord's coming" have to your real life?

> The Greek word from which KJV translators drew "effectual fervent" is energeo. It sounds a lot like our word energetic. It's active; it's intense; and therefore it's powerful.

2. The passage gives three practical pictures of patience: a farmer who waits for his crop; the prophets of the Old Testament who looked forward to Jesus' coming; and Job who persevered through unspeakable testing. Which of these resonates most with you? Why?

3. How do patience and perseverance integrate with the discussion in verse 9 about grumbling against fellow believers?

4. Recount what you can recall of Job's misfortune: its source, his response, his meeting with God, and his restoration. In what ways did Job persevere? What did the Lord bring about for this faithful servant? How does this encourage you in your struggle to persevere patiently?

5. What new understanding of perseverance do you gain in this passage that adds to what you observed in James 1:4?

6. What reminder does verse 11 give about God's character? How does this challenge you or empower you?

> Grousing and grumbling seldom accomplish anything positive. More often, they bring about disorder and discontent, ultimately derailing the mission. Instead, let's sow reconciliation and patience with one another, which leads to a united, forward-moving mission.

7. Why is it important to see God as both judge standing at the door, and provider of compassion and mercy, if we're to have an accurate understanding of who he is?

IMPLEMENT
(5–10 minutes)

Choose at least one activity to do before the next session. Tell one other person which item you chose.

1. In your quiet time with God, examine what Jesus said about his return. Read Matthew 24, paying attention to verse 14 where he makes a key statement: the gospel will be preached to every nation before the end comes. Find a way to participate in that mission starting today.

2. Ask God to show you instances where you've been grumbling or complaining against a fellow believer. Do everything you can to apologize and seek reconciliation.

3. Write the story of how you patiently endured a difficult circumstance God allowed in your life. Recall how God equipped you to withstand the pressure. Be real about your struggles and about the way God stepped into the situation alongside you. Use what you've written to encourage yourself and others to persevere through difficulties.

WRAP UP
(5 minutes)

As we draw our final session of *Celebrate James* to a close, Pastor Loy leaves us with some closing admonitions on prayer from the final verses of James.

Watch and listen to Session Twelve Part Two from the DVD.

Over these twelve sessions, James has challenged us to become more like our master Jesus Christ in the words that roll off our tongues, the deeds that give credence to our professed faith, and the interactions we have with fellow believers. In all this, the ultimate goal has been our maturity in Christ demonstrated in our joyfully serving him both now and forever.